uick
&
easy

Guinea Pig Care

T.F.H. Publications
One TFH Plaza
Third and Union Avenues
Neptune City, NJ 07753

ISBN 0-7938-1025-6

www.tfhpublications.com

Table of Contents

You and Your Guinea Pig

Congratulations on bringing home your guinea pig! You've just acquired a delightful, friendly pet that will bring you years of happiness and enjoyment.

Guinea pigs (also known as cavies) are lovable little animals, larger than hamsters but smaller than rabbits. They come in many different color combinations and have hair types ranging from short and smooth, to fuzzy, long, and even curly. Guinea pigs are very affectionate and develop close bonds with their owners. They love to snuggle and cuddle. Guinea pigs live longer than most other small pets. Their average lifespan is five years, but they may live as long as eight or even ten years. How well you care for your

Guinea pigs are lovable, friendly pets that are easy to care for.

pet will, in part, determine his longevity. Guinea pigs are naturally healthy animals and rarely become ill. Just because guinea pigs live in cages, it is wrong to assume that they have little or no requirements. On the contrary, guinea pigs need to be taken care of every day. They are relying on you to provide proper nutrition, a clean place to live, daily exercise, and lots of love. A guinea pig must have fresh food and water every day at regular times. He needs exercise and his cage should be cleaned daily.

Keeping your guinea pig happy and his home clean may seem like a lot of work, but when caring for your pet has become part of your everyday routine, you will find that it takes hardly any time at all. Providing for your new pet is easy to do, because these little creatures quickly capture your heart.

As a new owner of a guinea pig, be sure to set aside time each day to tend to your pet. After all, your new friend is depending on you for all of his or her basic care needs and should be treated with love and respect. Keep this in mind and you and your guinea pig will have many happy, healthy years together.

Your guinea pig is relying on you to provide for him for the rest of his life, and that is a big responsibility. Ask yourself the following questions to determine if you're ready, willing, and able to care for your pet properly:

1. Can I provide proper and continuous care for my guinea pig every day of his life?

2. Am I willing to let my pet live in the room in my home where I spend the most time, so that he will not be lonely?

3. Will I feed my guinea pig a healthy, balanced diet?

4. Will I give my pet fresh water every day?

5. Can I provide my guinea pig with a comfortable cage and a cozy nest box?

6. Will I remove all the soiled bedding from the cage every day?

7. Can I ensure that my guinea pig will be kept away from drafts, cold, too much heat or direct sunlight, cigarette smoke, and other pets that may harm him?

8. Do I have time to care for and give affection to my guinea pig every day?

9. Am I willing to groom my guinea pig regularly?

10. Do I have a place in my home where my guinea pig may exercise freely?

11. Is there a reliable caregiver available if I go away on vacation and cannot take my guinea pig with me?

What's in a Name?

The origin of the name guinea pig has been lost in antiquity, but a few theories have been put forward. When these little rodents first started to arrive in Britain during the 18th century, they were thought to have come from Guinea in West Africa. It is possible that they arrived from Guiana into northern South America. Another suggestion is they exchanged hands for one guinea—a princely sum in those days, having a value of one pound and one shilling.

The pig part is explained by the fact that people saw some sort of resemblance to an actual pig in the shape of its body and the squealing sounds that it makes. Cavy fanciers have adopted some "pig lingo" in their references to cavies. For example, male guinea pigs are called boars, female guinea pigs are called sows, pregnant guinea pigs are said to be "in-pig", and the babies are called piglets. Anyone who has ever owned a guinea pig has likely thought of their vocalizations as oinking. Thus, the cavy's nickname has stuck throughout the years.

12. Will I take my guinea pig to a vet if he needs medical attention?

13. Does my budget allow me to provide all the necessities that my guinea pig will require?

Guinea pigs have many attributes as pets and virtually no faults. They are small in size (most weigh about two pounds) and can be fed a wide range of inexpensive foods. Cavies are generally quiet, yet have a sufficient range of vocal tones to let you know how they are feeling. They are extremely clean in their personal habits and are never aggressive toward people or other animals.

Cavies and Other Pets

Cavies may get along fine with rabbits, provided that they are one of the smaller breeds. Other pets, such as dogs, cats, ferrets, and hedgehogs, are another matter. Generally, it is wise to keep your guinea pig away from them. These animals may decide that the guinea pig is a potential snack or at least something that can be played with, even if only in a friendly manner.

You will, of course, hear of people whose dogs and cats just love their guinea pig, but those whose pet has been killed or badly injured by these other pets will generally not boast about it. Play it safe and keep your guinea pig away from other pets.

Home Security

Guinea pigs need exercise, and you should allow your pet free access to one or more rooms in your home. A few safety tips are prudent. In warm weather, be careful that doors are not subject to drafts that might slam on the pet as he moves from one room to another. Be sure that all exterior doors and windows are closed when the guinea pig is roaming free. Warn other family members that the guinea pig is loose and they should be cautious about where they step and careful about opening and closing doors.

Consider bringing two guinea pigs into your home. They are social animals and will enjoy playing together.

If you bring your guinea pig's cage outdoors, be sure he cannot escape and that other animals cannot break into the cage.

Indoor plants should never be at floor level where the pet might nibble on them: some plants may be toxic to a guinea pig. Trailing electrical wires could be a source of danger if nibbled. Check each room to ensure that the guinea pig cannot get into a place in which you might have trouble retrieving him (such as behind the refrigerator or under a washing machine) or where other dangers might be present.

When exercising a guinea pig in your garden, do not give him access to flower beds that may have been sprayed with toxic chemicals, nor where other animals may have fouled the area with fecal matter. A guinea pig should never be left unsupervised outdoors. They have many potential enemies, such as dogs, cats, birds of prey, squirrels, and raccoons.

Vocalization and Temperament

A wide variety of vocalizations adds to the guinea pigs' appeal—they will frequently "talk" to you with squeals and chatters; their ears occasionally moving in rhythm with the sounds. Many guinea pigs will chatter and carry on from the moment you pick them up, making purring noises when scratched in just the right spot. Guinea pigs are alert and interested in what is happening around them, quickly learning to respond to the sound of your voice, whistle, or some other audible cue. Cavies soon learn to recognize your voice and will squeak and whistle with delight when it is dinnertime.

Quick & Easy Guinea Pig Care

How to Hold Your Cavy

Guinea pigs are heavier than they look and can move extremely fast. Unless the guinea pig is already hand tamed, he may display some initial fear of being handled. Never startle your pet as you approach him; do everything slowly and in such a way that the guinea pig is aware of your presence and your hands. It will probably scurry to a corner, at which time you can place one hand over its shoulders to steady him, placing the other hand under his body. It is important that his total weight is always supported by one hand; otherwise, he will feel insecure and start to wriggle. Never grasp him around his shoulders and lift so that his rear end is dangling unsupported.

If you handle your guinea pig for a few minutes each day he will become accustomed to the routine and look forward to snuggling with you.

A guinea pig's emotional well-being is as important as every other aspect of his health. These remarkable little animals are capable of

Always support your guinea pig's legs when lifting or holding him. Daily handling will tame your cavy.

feeling a variety of emotions, and they don't mind expressing them. Guinea pigs, just like people, can get lonely. Loneliness is an emotion that guinea pigs feel very easily, and they should not be expected to spend extended hours in seclusion. They need outside stimulation, exercise, human contact, and even toys. Some lonely guinea pigs become despondent and lose their zest for life even if they are in otherwise good health, while others will make desperate pleas for attention. A guinea pig that makes noise incessantly requires attention and is not squeaking simply to annoy you.

Guinea pigs respond with great excitement when something new is introduced into their small world. Something as simple as a piece of cardboard folded into a tent shape for them to run under makes for much amusement. An ecstatic guinea pig may do anything from squealing loudly to jumping, kicking, and running in circles quickly.

Owning a guinea pig is not only about you providing the best possible care for your pet; it is also about how your guinea pig can take care of you. Scientific research has proven that spending time with pets can reduce high blood pressure. Hugging your guinea pig will help you de-

Guinea Pig Vocabulary

Cavies have a variety of sounds they use to convey emotions. They "talk" with each other (and you) using a multitude of squeaks that sound like "wheeek", "wee-wee", or "drrr". They also employ loud teeth chattering, which is usually a sign of aggression or anger. Rumblestrutting or motorboating is a deep purr that the males use to show aggression or to assert dominance. A happy, excited guinea pig will jump and wiggle in the air; this is called popcorning. In no time at all, you will learn to understand what your cavy is trying to tell you. Your guinea pig will greet you at feeding time with enthusiasm and much vocalization.

stress, and their sweet, little faces are guaranteed to put a smile on your face. No other small pet will carry on a conversation with you the way a guinea pig does, and it doesn't matter that you don't speak the same language. The noises that guinea pigs make as you snuggle them are soothing, comforting sounds (especially the reassuring purr sound) that help to make your everyday cares disappear.

Housing Your Guinea Pig

Your guinea pig should feel at home in your home. Your cavy will spend a great deal of time in his cage, and it's important that the cage and furnishings provide your guinea pig with everything he needs to live a happy, healthy life.

Guinea pigs can be housed in a range of accommodations produced for rabbits and other small mammals. Visit a number of pet stores to see the widest range of cage options possible. The major requirements of good housing are that it is spacious, sturdy, secure, and easy to keep clean.

The Cage

Unfortunately, most pet animals, such as rabbits, hamsters, gerbils, mice, and guinea pigs, are kept in housing that is far too small to be regarded as adequate. The rule for guinea pig housing is that it should be as large as your finances will permit, and the larger the better. The minimum size should be about 24 x 15 inches (62 x 38cm). Such a cage will provide only enough room to serve as a sleeping and feeding facility. You must give your pet ample time outside of his cage in an outdoor exercise area or allow your guinea pig to roam freely in one room of your house. If two guinea pigs are to share the housing, the cage size should be increased by about 20 percent.

The cage should be ventilated on each of the four sides and the top and it should have a smooth, waterproof floor. Most cages have a top lid that latches securely, although this is only necessary to protect the pet from other animals. A guinea pig cannot leap out of his cage, nor is he physically capable of climbing up the sides.

Types of Cages

The most common type of guinea pig cage has sides made of wire bars that are fastened by clips to a plastic tray. The plastic tray is easy to clean and has high sides that help to prevent the bedding from being scattered by your pet.

Never house guinea pigs on a wire-mesh floor. Guinea pigs have bare feet with no padding and walking on wire is extremely uncomfortable. Walking on open wire bottoms is also dangerous to your pet. The guinea pig's small legs and toes can easily slip through the mesh, resulting in injury and permanent damage.

Another method of making things more comfortable is to feature wire mesh in one area, which, hopefully, the pet will use as a toilet, with the rest of the floor being solid. The guinea pig has small feet, and therefore, it is important that if mesh floors are a feature, there must be no danger of the guniea pig's nails getting tangled on the wire. Solid-floor cages are more comfortable, allow a generous layer of bedding to be used, and are a more natural surface on which to walk.

Where in the House?
After you purchase your guinea pig's cage, your next consideration should be where to place the cage in your home. Your guinea pig's cage should be located in a place appropriate for the pet's needs and yours. Remember that guinea pigs want to be where the action is.

Guinea pigs are curious animals. Place the cage in an area where the cavies can have interaction with members of your family.

Choose the Proper Cage

Remember that aquariums are designed for fish, not mammals. An aquarium tank is a bad choice for guinea pig housing; it is very poorly ventilated which will allow moisture to build up in the corners of the tank, and the smooth glass walls make it awkward to attach such necessities as food dishes, hay racks, and water bottles. Wooden hutches as used by rabbit breeders have largely been supplanted by the more airy and readily-cleaned cages previously discussed.

They are naturally curious and social animals, therefore you should place the cage in a location that is active and where you will spend most of your time. This way you can interact with your pet throughout the day.

The guinea pig's cage may sit on the floor or on a table—whatever is most convenient—but keep in mind that children must be able to reach the pet easily so that he may be lifted safely from the cage. Special consideration is needed if you have cats or dogs or other pets in the house. Make sure these pets can't get into the cage or knock it off the table.

A room that has natural light is a must, but never place a cage where it will receive direct sunlight, such as on a windowsill. The cage should not be facing doors where it could easily receive a draft during the colder months. Another poor location for the cage is over a radiator. There will be a temperature fluctuation as the appliances go on and off and this could easily induce chills. The best choice for cage placement is a light and airy location, where the temperature will be the most stable, yet where you can easily attend routine chores and observe your pet without any inconvenience.

The room temperature where you keep your guinea pig should be between 68° and 74°F and shouldn't fluctuate. Avoid exposing guinea pigs to cigarette smoke because it will irritate their delicate respiratory systems.

The Nest Box

Cavies are very shy creatures. In the wild, they keep a low profile by retreating behind rocks, in bushes, or under leaves when resting or sleeping. If this need to retreat is not met, it will greatly increase their stress level, making them more susceptible to illness.

You can easily overcome this risk by providing a small nest box or similar hiding place. A nest box is a like a little "house" inside the cage. Most guinea pigs also love to hop up on top of the nest box to perch and get a good view of their surroundings. You can purchase nest boxes from pet stores. When shopping, look for one that is at least 12 inches long, 9 inches wide, and 7 inches high—it should be much larger than the pig himself. The box should have a door on one side and preferably a small window on each of the other three sides for ventilation and viewing. Nest boxes can either be made of wood or chew-resistant plastic.

Ideally, a nest box should not have a floor. There are two reasons for this. The first is for easy access to your pet. When you want to handle your guinea pig, you can just lift the house up. The second reason is for easy cleaning. All you need to do is remove the house

Attention! Attention!

The more contact a guinea pig has with his family and the daily routine, the more his personality will develop. He will anticipate the arrival of the family and cheerfully greet anyone who stops by for a pat or snuggle. Therefore, the best location for your pet's home is in the room where the family spends the most time.

Housing Rabbits with Guinea Pigs

Although rabbits are more like guinea pigs than other small pets, it would be a mistake to assume that they always make good cage companions. While it is true that they get along well together and would rarely fight in most cases, the difference in size between a rabbit and a guinea pig may cause the guinea pig to feel intimidated. Often, a happy medium for both animals is impossible to achieve. Therefore, the best cagemate for a guinea pig is another guinea pig. If you think you'd like to try housing a small rabbit with your guinea pig, introduce the two of them and keep a watchful eye on them to see how they get along.

and clean the floor underneath as you would the rest of the cage. Plastic nest boxes have an advantage in that they can be washed with soap and water. Wooden nest boxes should have the bottom edges covered with waterproof tape to prevent urine from soaking into the wood. A small cardboard box makes a good temporary nest box. Cardboard is literally temporary, because guinea pigs love to chew cardboard and will eat themselves out of house and home in a few days.

Bedding

The best choices for floor covering include wood shavings, and natural wood or grass fiber. Aspen shavings are ideal bedding for guinea pig cages. Purchase only good-quality brands, and avoid aromatic blends. For maximum absorbency and comfort, a thick layer of shavings is needed in the cage. For guinea pig owners, purchasing shavings in small packages is not practical or economical. Pet stores sell shavings in large quantities or bales. Other types of bedding, such as ground corncob or pelleted litter made from recycled newspaper may be hard on the guinea pig's feet. Sheets of paper and granulated paper have good absorbency but are aesthetically unattractive. The ink in newsprint is potentially harmful.

Hay is a natural bedding and is one that the pet can also eat and use to make a small nest area. However, when damp from urine, water, or fecal matter, it may quickly spawn fungi. This is its biggest drawback, along with the fact that it has limited absorbency. Hay should never smell musty, nor show signs of mold.

Cedar shavings must never be used as a bedding material for any small animal. High content of fragrant oils (phenols) naturally present in cedar shavings causes eye, respiratory, and skin irritations in guinea pigs. Sawdust is too fine and can create problems if it sticks to the anogenital region or the swollen teats of a nursing sow. It can cling to the guinea pig's eyes, coat, and nasal passages, causing much discomfort. Sawdust can also get into the guinea pig's soft foods, such as mashes or fruits and vegetables and can be quite messy. Straw has little absorbency, and its sharp ends can be injurious to the eyes of these pets. Sand is a poor choice because it can stain the coats of the guinea pigs and is also an irritant.

Shavings

Shavings are the most popular and economical bedding for guinea pigs. Never obtain shavings from sawmills or lumberyards. They may contain mites and other unwanted parasites. Purchase commercially bagged shavings from your pet shop. Some are impregnated with chlorophyll (giving a green color) to reduce odors and make them more attractive. You will find that some shavings are more dust free than others—their extra cost is worth it on this account. The depth of bedding should be about 2 inches (5cm).

Cleaning the Cage

When considering the health of your guinea pig, there is no substitute for daily cage cleaning—a deodorizer must not be used to mask

Keep your cavy's cage clean, he will thank you for it.

uncleanliness. An unpleasant aroma in your home from an unclean cage is not the guinea pig's fault, but the result of poor cage maintenance on your part. Guinea pig droppings are firm and oblong in shape and, when dry, are hard and odorless. The urine has a milky appearance, and odor from it builds up only if the damp bedding is not removed. All soiled bedding must be removed every day, and fresh bedding should be added to replace that which you have taken out.

Some guinea pigs are tidy housekeepers and only mess in one or two corners of their cage. Regardless of how neat the guinea pig is, the bedding should be completely replaced once a week and the cage floor scrubbed. For regular cleaning, use a solution of vinegar and water or dish detergent. If disinfection is required, try not to use a formula with a really strong fragrance, and be sure to rinse it off thoroughly. A scrub pad or toothbrush is good for cleaning the corners of the cage.

Make sure the cage is dry before adding clean bedding. To increase the absorbency of the bedding, you may choose to place an additional lining underneath, such as cardboard or newspaper.

Exercise and the Great Outdoors

Pet guinea pigs are not really meant to live outdoors and should not be kept in a barn, shed, or garage. They are extremely susceptible to chills, drafts, and dampness and like to be kept warm and cozy inside your house with you.

However, there is nothing guinea pigs like better than to spend a few hours outdoors on warm spring and summer days. They love fresh air and sunshine and will devour grass as if they are starving. Exercise not only keeps the cavy in a fit and healthy condition, but it is essential for their psychological well-being. Guinea pigs do not like being imprisoned in a cage for long periods any more than you would enjoy being restricted to a single room for days on end. This

Provide your guinea pig with a nest box so he has a place to retreat from the world.

Guinea pigs need daily exercise. Your cavy will enjoy spending a few hours outdoors with you in a protected area.

type of confinement results in stress, and stress greatly increases the chances of ill health.

If you live in an area with ample yard space you can take your cavy outside for some exercise and a change of scenery. However, a few precautions are required.

You need to provide a secure pen that restricts the guinea pig from wandering away, and will not allow potential intruders, such as dogs or cats, to enter. Never let your guinea pig wander outside without an enclosure. It's a very big and dangerous world out there for a little pig that is used to being enclosed by four safe walls.

Construction of an outdoor run is simple. You may want a long, narrow run (say 6 feet long by 2 feet wide and 12 inches high) or something more square. Almost any size will do, but the run should be easy to move around the yard, so that your pet can have a fresh grazing area each time out. A wood frame covered with hardware

Quick & Easy Guinea Pig Care

cloth (the wire that's made up of little squares) on all four sides and on the top is adequate. (Any wood you use must not be painted or chemically treated. Avoid using chipboard and particleboard for the safety of the guinea pig that likes to gnaw.) There should be a hiding spot in one corner. This will allow the guinea pig to retreat from the sun if he becomes too warm. A hinged door with a secure latch is also required. The outdoor enclosure can be equipped with rocks and plastic tunnels for your cavy to play in and around.

Outdoor Safety Precautions

Never put your guinea pig out on damp grass, in rain, strong winds, near loud noises or working lawn mowers, or if it is below 61° F. Don't place an outdoor enclosure on chemically treated lawns or in areas where other pets may have visited. Always place the outdoor enclosure where there is access to some shade, (half sun, half shade is best), and remember that the sun moves, so keep checking on your pet. Guinea pigs should not stay out for extended periods on really hot days. They should have access to cool, fresh water at all

Cavies like to explore different surroundings. Let your guinea pig get the exercise he needs while he satisfies his natural curiosity.

Guinea pigs should never be left outside unattended. Make sure to keep a close eye on your pet while he is outdoors.

times. Don't leave home while your guinea pig is outside unattended, and never leave him out overnight.

Indoor Exercise

If you are not able to create an outdoor exercise run for your guinea pig, there are several ways you can provide him with indoor exercise. Exercise wheels are very useful accessories for guinea pigs, but they must be large enough and safe. Avoid those with open treads, through which the cavy's legs or toes can easily become trapped. You need to buy an exercise wheel with a solid non-slip floor. It should be sturdy, so that it will not easily topple over. Always remember that it pays to invest in the best cage accessories. They are safer and will give you much longer wear. Pet stores will also sell appropriately sized plastic tubes secured onto a flat plastic base, or ones that can be made into small tunnels. These will work fine and provide amusement for your guinea pig.

Feeding and Nutrition

Guinea pigs are herbivores, so they eat no meat or animal products in the wild. This means that their diet consists exclusively of plant and vegetable matter. It is essential that they have a high-fiber, low-fat-content diet rich in vitamin C. Guinea pigs cannot synthesize vitamin C and any deficiency will result in poor health.

Feeding your guinea pig a proper diet will ensure his health, happiness, longevity, and overall condition. Two components make up a guinea pig's diet: dry foods—prepared guinea pig food and hay; and fresh vegetables and fruit that must include a source of vitamin C.

Dry Foods
Pellets

Guinea pig pellets are alfalfa-based and contain the necessary vitamins and minerals that provide the foundation for your pet's nutrition. Buy only pellets made specifically for guinea pigs. Hamster or rabbit food or combination small animal mixes are not suitable for guinea pigs. They lack essential vitamin C and may contain ingredients guinea pigs cannot easily digest. Purchase a good-quality brand of pellet from a reputable pet food manufacturer. Check the label—dehydrated alfalfa should be the first ingredient listed. Gourmet blends of pelleted food with dehydrated fruit, vegetables, and nuts are also available, but they aren't necessary to provide balanced nutrition. The added ingredients can cause some guinea pigs intestinal discomfort and distract them from consuming the nutritious pellets. For optimum freshness, purchase pellets in sealed bags and not from bulk bins. Don't buy pellets in quantities larger than what can be used up in a few weeks and use airtight containers for storing them.

Before you run out of pellets, purchase a new bag and mix some of those pellets in with your current supply over a period of a few days, even if you are feeding the same brand of food. There may be a slight difference in the ingredients used to manufacture each

Pellets

Guinea pigs should be fed pellets on a free-choice basis—that is, there should always be some in the food dish. Try to put only about as many pellets in the dish as your pet will eat in one day. Any uneaten pellets should be removed before adding more, because guinea pigs will not eat stale pellets. Also, make sure the pellets do not become damp, because they quickly turn moldy.

Quick & Easy Guinea Pig Care

Always provide your guinea pig with fresh vegetables as part of his regular diet.

batch of pellets, and that could cause the guinea pig intestinal upset. Gradually mixing in the new food helps to prevent this.

Hay

Hay is an important part of a guinea pig's diet and should be available at all times. It aids in the digestion of food, and guinea pigs love it! Hay is especially beneficial to longhaired breeds in helping to prevent hairballs, and to all guinea pigs in helping to minimize the risk of diarrhea. It is better to feed hay made from timothy grass or a combination of alfalfa and other mixed grasses rather than pure alfalfa. Alfalfa is acceptable but is richer in calories and calcium. Large amounts of pure alfalfa may cause bloating in guinea pigs. Purchase only high-quality hay. Poor hay that is moldy or dusty is very harmful to guinea pigs. Never feed hay that looks "off" or smells other than fresh. It will cause stomach upsets. Store hay in a cool dry area that is well ventilated to avoid fungal spores from developing.

Feeding and Nutrition

Treats

There are many different kinds of treats available. Buy only those made especially for guinea pigs, and feed them in small amounts so that your pet will not be discouraged from eating his regular food. If you choose to offer sunflower seeds or peanuts to your guinea pig, be sure to remove the shells first, because the sharp bits are a choking hazard.

Guinea pigs will eat a large handful of hay each day that should be supplied from a rack and not thrown on the cage floor where it will be soiled. Any hay that ends up on the cage floor must be removed as part of your daily cleaning. Always carefully sift through each handful of hay before placing it in the rack. Even the best-quality hay may have the occasional thistle mixed in with it. Thistles must be removed, because they will injure the guinea pig's mouth.

Seeds and Grain

The grain part of the menu is usually crushed oats and bran, but flaked maize and any other grain crops can be fed to your pets. The by-products of these, such as breakfast cereals and bread, can also be included. Although guinea pigs will enjoy grain, it should only be fed as a treat and not as a staple diet. Grain lacks the proper balanced nutrition of prepared foods, and too much tends to cause obesity. Guinea pigs will eat many cereal crops, together with seeds such as canary and sunflower. As with many food items, your pet may be selective. If you are feeding hay, pellets, and mixed plants, care should be exercised in the feeding of high-protein and high-carbohydrate seeds and grain.

Toasted or baked bread is beneficial for guinea pigs as it provides a hard food that will help keep their teeth in good shape. Baked bread, pellets, and small branches of fruit and other edible trees are required to ensure your pet's teeth stay at the required length. If a guinea pig does not have hard items on which to gnaw, his incisor teeth will grow to an excessive length, which creates major problems.

Food cubes are hard and flavorful and help promote the natural wearing of the teeth. These may be fed as a treat, but not on a daily basis. They contain animal protein that will cause your guinea pig to gain too much weight.

Fresh Foods

Each guinea pig has his own special set of taste buds and will show specific likes and dislikes for different kinds of food. If a cavy has made up his mind not to eat something, there is not much you can do to convince him otherwise.

A cardinal rule that should be adhered to when feeding guinea pigs is that the food should always be clean and fresh. Fresh foods, such as greens or fruits, should not be overripe, nor left exposed to flies. Always wash such foods before feeding them to your pets.

Never leave fresh foods down for the guinea pig to eat for longer than one day. Any food that is uneaten after this time should be discarded. Uneaten mashes cannot be stored after they have been served to your pets. They should be mixed fresh for each serving,

Small Portions, Please

Although guinea pigs always appear ravenous, they do not eat to the point of gluttony. Guinea pigs feast only until they are full, and any uneaten food must be removed from the cage every day. To avoid waste, feed your guinea pig a small handful of fresh vegetables and fruit two or three times a day, preferably at regular intervals, rather than a large amount at once.

and any excess placed in the refrigerator to be used the following day. Food taken from the fridge should be fully thawed before being served.

Fresh foods may be served from a separate feeding rack or be set on the nest box, but guinea pigs tend to pull the tasty morsels to the floor and devour them quickly. A small pet dish placed on the cage floor makes a good server for fresh foods. It should be removed from the cage and washed after each feeding.

Vegetables and fruits with the richest colors contain the most food value. Mix a small salad for the guinea pigs and watch which foods they obviously like best; these will be the ones eaten first.

Cavies like to eat fresh fruits and vegetables which are an important source of vitamin C.

Quick & Easy Guinea Pig Care

Give your guinea pig a variety of vegetables and fruits. He will let you know which ones are his favorites.

The vitamin C and fiber content of green leaf plants make them excellent supplements to hay and pellets. They also provide high moisture content. Never give your guinea pig any food that has even the slightest bit of mold on it. Mold is fatal to guinea pigs. Do not feed your pet any food that is spoiled. (If you wouldn't eat it, your pet shouldn't either.) The importance of not feeding any of these foods in excess cannot be overstressed. It is also wise to rinse all plants, vegetables, and fruits to remove residual chemicals used in crop spraying.

Guinea Pigs' Favorite Foods
The following is a list of foods that most guinea pigs will eat:

Lettuce—Feed only Romaine or green leaf lettuce. Iceberg (or head lettuce) contains mostly fiber and water and has little nutritional value for guinea pigs.

Kale and spinach—These are especially rich in vitamin C.

Grass—Grass is one food guinea pigs never seem to grow tired of, whether they are picking it themselves outside or munching on some you have brought in for them. Do not pick grass from roadsides or from lawns that have been sprayed with chemicals or used by other pets. Never feed clippings that have been mulched through a lawnmower.

Dandelion leaves and clover—Feed in small amounts and also be careful where you pick them.

Carrots—Peel and trim off both ends, some cavies may like the leafy carrot tops.

Broccoli—Guinea pigs will also eat the stock part.

Cucumber—The most food value is contained in the peelings. (Some cucumbers sold in grocery stores are heavily waxed. These peelings should not be fed to guinea pigs.)

Melons (watermelon, cantaloupe, and honey dew)—Remove the seeds. Guinea pigs also enjoy the rinds.

Also: Apples, celery (especially the leaves), Swiss chard, parsley, endive.

Other Foods

Then there is the alternative list of foods that are worth trying even though some guinea pigs may refuse them: shepherd's purse, groundsel, chickweed, plantain, bramble, clover, coltsfoot, mallow, chard, tomatoes, green peppers, citrus fruit, strawberries, pineapple (good natural sources of vitamin C); pea pods, grapes, bananas, pears, peas, corn husks (but not the stringy "tassel" parts). Cabbage may be offered in small amounts. Most guinea pigs will enjoy gnawing on vegetable cores such as those from lettuce and celery, but do not feed them fruit cores because they may choke on the seeds.

Never feed your guinea pig the following: houseplants of any kind, junk food, candy or sweets, beans, any part of the potato plant itself including potato peelings, any part of the tomato plant itself, beet leaves, rhubarb, flowers or any part of any flowering plant, unknown weeds, or any foods that have been previously frozen. If you are unsure about a particular wild plant, do not feed it. Never feed any plant grown from a bulb. If in doubt, don't feed it to your guinea pig!

Vitamin C

Guinea pigs, like humans, cannot manufacture their own vitamin C. Many of the health problems that affect guinea pigs can be traced to vitamin C deficiencies. Feeding your pet a proper, balanced diet maintains good nutrition, but providing a daily supplement of vitamin C ensures that your guinea pig is consuming an adequate amount. While all guinea pig pellets are fortified with vitamin C, it should be noted that this vitamin is difficult to stabilize and deteriorates as the food is stored. While the food itself is still fresh, the vitamin C content may have become depleted. Sufficient amounts of vitamin C are essential

Kitchen Safety

The same food bacteria that make people sick (such as salmonella and *E. coli*) can also seriously harm a guinea pig. Therefore, when preparing your pet's fresh foods, be careful to place them only on clean counter tops and cutting boards. Do not store vegetables in the refrigerator next to raw meat packets that may leak juices and cause contamination.

for the development of young, growing guinea pigs, especially in the formation of bones. A well-balanced, carefully prepared diet containing fruits and vegetables should provide the necessary vitamin C your cavy needs.

Mashes

You can concoct any number of recipes in order to prepare a mash for your pets. The basic ingredients will be crushed oats and bran. To these you can add such items as chopped boiled eggs, grated cheese, nuts and seeds, and assorted chopped fruits and vegetables. Mix these all together in a bowl, and then add just a little warm water. This should only be enough to bring the ingredients together so the mash is moist, not a sloppy mess! You can even add honey. Try a few experimental mashes and let your guinea pig choose the one he prefers.

Salt Licks

Salt licks are available in two colors—white and brown. The brown ones are a better choice, because they also contain trace minerals that help to maintain your guinea pig's overall health. Circular in shape, a salt lick has a hole in the center for fastening it to the cage and can be held in place with wire or string. Once your pet has licked his way to the middle, the salt lick needs to be replaced, because it will no longer stay secured to the cage.

Water

Your guinea pig should have access to fresh, clean water at all times. Most people pay little attention to the quality of water supplied to their pets. This is because we all assume water is water, and it is safe providing it is from the faucet. However, the quality of water does differ significantly from one region, or country, to another. What might not adversely affect our health may well affect animals that are much smaller. In their case, excess quantities of certain chemicals can cause problems. If you live in an area that treats the water with many chemicals you should consider giving your pet filtered or bottled water.

Food and Water Containers

Food Dishes

The most functional dishes for serving dry foods to guinea pigs are those that can be attached to the cage. These are made of stainless steel or plastic and have hangers on the back that are placed through the cage wire. These dishes are found in pet stores and are easily cleaned with soap and water. (Remember to rinse thoroughly.)

Guinea pigs should always have a source of fresh water available. A water bottle is the easiest way to provide your cavy with the water he needs.

Other choices, such as heavy ceramic pots that sit on the cage floor won't work as efficiently with guinea pigs. Even if the pot is too heavy to tip over, your pet will undoubtedly sit in the dish and soil it. Also, having the food dish off the cage floor will give your pet more room to move about.

Water Bottles

Water is the only beverage a guinea pig needs, and there must be a fresh, constant supply. A plastic water bottle designed especially for small animals is the only practical and functional way of providing water for your guinea pig. These bottles are fastened to the cage with a wire ring. They have a metal sipper tube with a small ball inside that regulates the flow of water as your pet drinks and prevents the bottle from dripping constantly. Any other means of watering your pet, such as placing a bowl inside the cage, will not work because the bowl will be tipped over or soiled. Never give your guinea pig any kind of

Vitamin Supplements

There are many protein, vitamin, and mineral supplements available today—not all necessarily packaged for guinea pigs. If you feed your pets a wide-ranging diet that already includes proteins, vitamins, and carbohydrates, you should have no need to supply concentrated supplements. An excess of any vitamin or mineral can be harmful to your pet, because it upsets the absorption rate of other compounds.

If you feel that your guinea pig shows some other symptom that may suggest nutritional deficiency, discuss the matter with your vet before you purchase any supplements. Vitamins should be supplied only under the advice of a vet after he or she has examined your pet.

drinking device that has a glass sipper tube. Guinea pigs tend to gnaw on their sipper tubes rather vigorously, and a glass one would severely injure your pet if he gnaws through it.

All guinea pigs have different drinking habits. Some will drink a lot of water and others hardly any, though most will consume large amounts in warm weather. There are different sizes of water bottles available—an eight-ounce bottle is usually large enough for one guinea pig. You must replenish your guinea pig's water every day. Fill the water bottle to capacity so that a vacuum can be formed in the bottle, thereby preventing water from dripping out of the sipper tube.

Water bottles should be washed with soap and water daily. They are prone to algae buildup, and some guinea pigs blow water back into the bottle as they drink, allowing food particles to get inside. Use a very small amount of dish soap, hot water, and a bottlebrush to scrub inside the plastic bottle. Wash inside the lid and clean inside the sipper tube with a cotton swab. Rinse thoroughly. Be sure to position the bottle so your guinea pig can easily reach it.

Feeding Your Guinea Pig
When to Feed

It is not important when your guinea pigs are fed during the day as long as you stick to a set time. They are creatures of habit, and look forward to their food on time. They will show their anticipation of their meals by running around giving out high-pitched squeaks when you approach. The best time to feed fresh foods and mashes are first thing in the morning or in the late afternoon. Supplying such foods at these times reduces the risk of it souring during the hot midday period. Oats, bran, and pellets can be supplied more or less on an ad-lib basis, so it is simply a case of topping up their dish as it is emptied.

How Much to Feed?

Guinea pigs need sufficient food to meet their health and activity level. A large pet will clearly eat more than will a small one. An active guinea pig given plenty of exercise will burn up more energy than will a guinea pig in a small cage.

Given these different needs, and the fact that some foods are more nutritious than others, it is not possible to state exact amounts to feed. The best way to determine quantity is to supply a given amount of pellets, mixed grain, and fresh foods (plus unlimited hay) and see how much of it is eaten within a few hours.

Guinea pigs like to be fed at the same time every day. They will anxiously await their meals.

If all or most is eaten, you can increase the quantity of those items completely eaten at the next meal. If a lot is left, you can reduce the amount. The ideal situation is that in which the guinea pig eats most of his food, but some is left to be eaten later. By such an adjustment method, you will soon arrive at the optimum for good health and minimal waste.

Feeding Philosophy

Feeding any form of livestock is not a science, though a basic understanding of the role of various foods is beneficial. It is more a matter of applying common sense and ensuring the food represents a balance of items that are fed in a fresh state. Never be afraid to experiment with food items to see if your pets like them. If your guinea pig appears to be obese, do not withhold food. The remedy to the problem is to reduce the quantity.

Where feeding is concerned, everything should be done gradually, so the guinea pig's digestive system is never subjected to sudden changes. When you obtain your guinea pig, be sure to ask what his present diet is. If it is not balanced, make changes gradually. This will enable the pet's digestive system to slowly adjust to the new feeding regimen. Problems, if any, will be minor and should clear up within a few days.

Observe Your Pet at Mealtimes

Always take the time to watch your guinea pig when he is eating. You will learn much about his habits, including what foods he prefers. Any change in the guinea pig's eating habits may be the first sign of a problem.

If your pet is receiving a balanced diet, he will display good body substance, being neither fat nor thin. He will be alert and active and will display an obviously healthy coat. If your guinea pig does not present this kind of appearance, or stops eating for any reason, you should seek veterinary advice.

Grooming Your Guinea Pig

Brushing

All guinea pigs benefit from daily brushing, and for the longhaired breeds, it is absolutely essential to keep the coat healthy, shiny and free from tangles. Daily grooming also encourages bonding between you and your guinea pig and helps you to keep a watchful eye on your pet's health. You will be able to detect any subtle changes that could be cause for concern.

Pet stores sell a variety of soft-bristled brushes, slickers, and combs for small animals. Rough-coated guinea pigs can be brushed in any direction—they always seem to be having a bad hair day! Some smooth-coated guinea pigs like to have their hair brushed backward, but most will protest at being rubbed the wrong way, preferring soft, gentle strokes in the natural direction of the hair. Putting a few drops of water on your hands and rubbing it into the coat before brushing will help to dislodge any loose hair. Guinea pigs shed a small amount, and this may occur at any time of the year. Since guinea pigs have natural oils present in their hair, grooming brushes should be washed with shampoo occasionally.

Smoothcoated guinea pigs hardly need grooming, as their coat will stay in sparkling condition. Even so, you should groom them at least once a week as this helps them to get used to being handled. Always place your pet on a firm, non-slip surface when grooming. You can use a soft brush to gently remove any small bits of debris that may be clinging to the coat. If you are gentle they will enjoy this massage. Finish the job with a soft piece of cloth, or a chamois, which will leave the coat with a glossy sheen.

The longcoated varieties, such as Shelties and Peruvians, must be groomed every other day, at least, if their coat is to remain in a mat free state. Give the coat a brisk brushing to remove debris and some of the tangles. Next, use a medium width comb and gently groom the fur. Do not pull on tangles, but tease them apart with your fingers, then brush them, and then comb again. By using this progressive method of grooming you will greatly reduce the risk of hurting the guinea pig.

Bathing
Other than the longcoated varieties, your guinea pig may never need

A Quick Check

While grooming your pet, check his ears and body for any signs of parasites, abrasions, or growths. You can also check that his teeth are in good shape, and that his nails are not overgrown.

Quick & Easy Guinea Pig Care

Daily brushing helps you bond with your guinea pig. Most cavies enjoy it.

to be bathed. However, sometimes an individual may get himself in a mess, especially the lighter-colored individuals and the roughcoated varieties, whose fur more readily gathers dirt. Bathing should always be done on warm days, and as early in the day as possible. This allows plenty of time for your pet to dry before the evening.

Guinea pigs are best bathed in a sink that has a flat bottom, such as the kitchen sink or a laundry tub. Put a towel on the bottom of the sink so the guinea pig has soft, secure footing, and do not fill the sink because your pet will be terrified of drowning.

Bathing Procedures

Dampen the pig slowly and gently with warm (not hot) water, using a dipper from a pail or your hand. Try not to splash your pet and

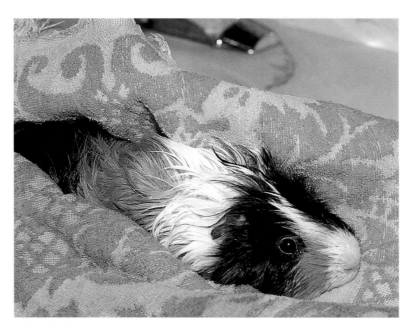

If you bathe your guinea pig, use warm water and mild soap. Be sure to dry your guinea pig thoroughly so he doesn't get a chill.

never pour water on the guinea pig's head—the water must not be allowed to run into the cavy's nose or ears. Gently folding down the flaps of the ears will help keep out soap and water when you are working around the head and neck. Dilute the shampoo with a little water and work it into the coat, avoiding the eyes and ears. The face can be cleaned later with a damp cloth. A soft toothbrush is useful for washing shorter coats. Avoid scrubbing longhaired guinea pigs to prevent the hair from tangling—gently work the shampoo through the hair with your fingers instead. Some guinea pigs may actually enjoy baths, but most try to think of ways to escape from the sink. Always keep one hand on the pig to prevent him from trying to jump out. A soapy guinea pig is extremely slippery! Rinse your guinea pig thoroughly with warm, clean water, making sure that all soap residue is removed.

When you have finished rinsing, quickly wrap the guinea pig in a thick terry towel to absorb excess water and then use a handheld

Keeping your guinea pig well-groomed will allow you to bond with your pet and keep him happy and healthy.

Grooming Your Guinea Pig

hair dryer on a low setting to complete drying. Be careful when using the hair dryer on your cavy, the loud noise and sudden heat may frighten him. Most wet pigs will gladly welcome the warm air blowing on their fur. For safety, hold the hair dryer several inches away from your pet and use a rapid motion when drying so that the warm air is not allowed to blow on one spot for more than a few seconds at a time. Make sure your guinea pig is thoroughly dry before returning him to his cage. Do not allow your guinea pig outdoors until you are certain he is completely dry.

Ear Care

A guinea pig's ears are small, thin flaps of skin with scarcely any hair covering them. Behind each ear is a bald spot. The ears will sometimes get very hot and pink ears may turn red. They can also get quite cold. These hairless ears possibly play a part in helping the guinea pig regulate his body temperature. Clean your guinea pig's ears about once a month or after bathing to remove any stray droplets of water.

To clean the ears, apply a small amount of mineral oil to a cotton ball. With your pet placed securely on your lap, gently and carefully clean inside the grooves and folds of the ear with a swab. Never push the swab deep into the ear canal. Some guinea pigs dislike having their ears cleaned, but most will find it soothing. Guinea pigs aren't very far from the ground, and because their ears offer little in the way of protection, it is easy for dust, dirt, and other particles to get trapped inside. Cleaning the ears also removes the wax that is naturally present inside. Lightly pigmented ears have pale yellow wax inside them, while darker ears have wax that is nearly black in color.

Nail Care

Guinea pigs have four toes on their front feet and three toes on their back feet. The toenails must be kept trimmed, for your sake as well as your pet's. Because a guinea pig walks on his toes, long nails will impair his ability to move correctly. On hard floors, a guinea pig

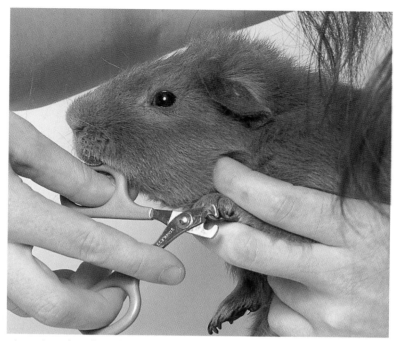

A cavy's nails will need to be trimmed from time to time. Your veterinarian can show you how to do this yourself.

with long nails will not have any traction, and on carpets, long nails may catch and tear. Trim the nails about once a month to prevent them from splitting and breaking.

If you are not sure how to go about trimming the nails, ask a veterinarian to show you. Small, guillotine-type clippers or ordinary nail clippers will do the job. Avoid using scissors because they may cause the nails to split. Inside the toenail is blood and tissue called the quick. Try not to cut into this. The quick is easily seen on guinea pigs with white nails. On darker nails it is not so easy to tell where the quick is, so trim only the tips if you are nervous about cutting too far. As a precaution, you can purchase styptic powder to stop any bleeding quickly if you accidentally cut the quick.

To cut the nails, hold the guinea pig around his middle and close to your side. Proceed to clip the nails. If the guinea pig is being

Grooming Your Guinea Pig

uncooperative, place him on a table and have someone else hold him securely while you clip the nails. The guinea pig will be nervous and may protest at first, but with lots of reassurance, nail trimming will get easier for both you and your pet.

Special Care for Boars

It is very important to make sure that your boar stays clean underneath. Uncleanliness can result in irritation or even infection of the genitals. Boars are not always good at cleaning themselves, so they may require some help from you. Check the boar's underside daily to make sure there are no problems. If the boar's genital area looks dirty or has bits of bedding stuck to it you can gently wash the area with warm water.

The Oil Gland

An oil-producing gland, sometimes called the grease spot, is located at the base of the tailbone, where the tail would be. This gland is found on both genders, but it is most prominent and active in adult boars. The secretions from this gland allow the guinea pig to mark territory with a special scent that only other guinea pigs can smell. The result is a buildup of a dark, sticky, wax-like substance. Guinea pigs cannot reach this spot themselves, so the area must be washed when the "grease" builds up to prevent irritation. The grease spot may need to be cleaned every few weeks, depending on the individual guinea pig. Use a mild shampoo and gently loosen the "grease" with your fingertips. It is not necessary to bathe the entire pig—just hold him securely under the belly with one hand, dampen his back end, wash, and rinse. Shampoo may need to be reapplied to clean the area completely. Towel-dry and comb out the hairs and then you are done!

Guinea Pig Health Care

Guinea pigs do not have much built-in immunity to help them fight off an illness once it strikes. If you suspect that your guinea pig is ill, do not wait to see if the problem goes away on its own, take him to the veterinarian. A guinea pig has the best chance of recovery when treatment is provided at the first sign of illness.

Choosing a Veterinarian

It is as important for guinea pigs to have annual checkups as it is for dogs and cats to receive vaccinations. Regular checkups help prevent potential health problems so your pet can live longer. Choosing a veterinarian for your guinea pig is not a task to be taken lightly. Not all vets are equipped with the knowledge and skill needed to care for a guinea pig. Therefore, you need to seek out an exotic animal specialist. These vets not only treat guinea pigs but other pet rodents, birds, and reptiles. If you live in a small town, you may have to go to the nearest city to locate an exotic animal specialist.

Antibiotics

Guinea pigs have delicate digestive systems containing special microorganisms that help them digest their food. Common antibiotics, especially those containing penicillin, are toxic to guinea pigs. There are only a few safe antibiotics for guinea pigs, but these are usually quite effective. Only your veterinarian should administer any medications or antibiotics to your guinea pig.

Causes of Disease in Guinea Pigs

While a disease can suddenly strike your pet almost without warning, this situation is actually uncommon. The problem may be

Not all veterinarians treat guinea pigs. Be sure to find an exotic animal specialist in your area.

Quick & Easy Guinea Pig Care

Finding an Exotic Animal Specialist

Owners of small mammals (such as guinea pigs) need to take their pets to veterinarians experienced and trained in treating "exotic" pets. There are several ways you can locate a vet who sees guinea pigs. For starters, check your telephone directory. Veterinarians who treat exotics should be listed. If none are listed, call a veterinarian's office or animal clinic and ask if someone can refer you to an exotic animal specialist. The pet shop or breeder where you purchased your guinea pig should also be able to provide you with a local vet who treats guinea pigs.

caused by conditions that enabled the pathogenic (disease causing) organisms to reproduce in large numbers to the point that they overwhelmed the natural defense mechanisms of your guinea pig.

Lack of Quarantine

This is one of the greatest causes of problems with those who own two or more guinea pigs or who own other pets such as rabbits, and then add guinea pigs to their collection. When you purchase an additional animal, regardless of how good his former home was, you cannot be sure whether or not he happens to be incubating some illness. If he is, any other pet he comes into contact with will quickly contract this ailment.

You should keep all newly acquired stock isolated from other pets for a period of about twenty-one days. During this time, you can monitor the new pet's feeding habits and gradually make any necessary changes to his diet. This time will also allow the new pet to make the adjustment from his former home without the added stress that might be caused by placing him with other animals. It will, at this time, encounter bacteria that are local to your area. If these adversely affect him they should do so during the quarantine period.

Take the new pet to the veterinarian for a check up as soon as possible and have your vet do a fecal analysis to see if there are signs of excess worm eggs.

Lack of Hygiene

This subject covers everything from daily and weekly cleaning of the cage, to correct storage of foods and personal hygiene. It also means keeping the stockroom and its adjacent areas spotlessly clean and free of any form of garbage that could house pathogens or their hosts, such as mice or rats.

Cracked and chipped food and water containers should be discarded and replaced as soon as damage is noticed. All feeding utensils and dishes should be washed daily.

It is important that you always wash your hands before handling your pet, and especially if:

1. You have visited a friend who owns guinea pigs or other rodent pets.

2. You have been gardening without wearing rubber gloves.

3. You have just handled a guinea pig that is, or is suspected to be, ill.

4. You have visited a guinea pig show or another show where various livestock are on display. It is easy to transport pathogens into your home via your hands or clothing.

Feeding Unfresh Foods

While the life of dry foods, such as oats and pellets, is relatively long, this only applies if they are kept in a dry state. Even so, it is not wise to store foods for any length of time. Greenfoods (fresh fruits and vegetables) readily deteriorate and will spoil faster in

Good hygiene habits and a clean cage will prevent many health problems and keep your guinea pig happy.

warmer months. Discard any food that smells bad or you suspect may be spoiled.

Overcrowding

Obviously, the more guinea pigs that are placed in a single cage, the greater the risk of direct contact transmission of illness or disease. If the guinea pigs are cramped for space, they are more likely to squabble and suffer injury from fighting. This induces stress, thus increasing the risk of illness. Always provide your pet with ample room to run about and play inside the cage.

Stress

Stress is a condition that is very difficult to pinpoint and is a major precursor of problems and illnesses in pets. This is especially so in guinea pigs, which are by nature very shy and nervous little animals.

Stress can affect your guinea pig in three ways. It can induce abnormal behavior patterns, can reduce the performance of the immune system, and can reduce the pet's ability to correctly utilize vitamin C.

Delay in Responding to Visual Signs of Illness

Once you suspect that your guinea pig is not well, do not wait for matters to get worse before you react. Contact your vet, who will be able to tell you, based on the information that you supply, whether you need to visit the clinic as soon as possible.

As a general precaution, if you suspect an illness it is wise to move the pet's cage to an area where it is a little warmer and quieter. If diarrhea is evident, withhold moist foods pending advice from the vet, but maintain the water supply.

If the clinical signs seem serious, gather some fecal samples in a plastic container and place them in the refrigerator (never the freezer). Your vet may want them for microscopic examination. If your guinea pig is clearly ill, you will need to completely clean his cage and discard bedding and any twigs or other soft items. Hygiene now becomes especially important, so be sure to wash your hands before and after handling the pet.

Know your guinea pig—his quirks, his mannerisms, and his sounds; what is normal and what is not for your pet. The slightest change in behavior could indicate the onset of an illness. Any pattern of behavior that you have never noticed before should be viewed with suspicion. Sometimes behavioral signs will be the only visual indicators of a problem. For this reason, it is important that you spend time observing your pet when he is eating. You can establish whether he is a greedy or dainty eater, what foods are his favorites, and how often and how much he drinks.

If signs of illness are observed, it could indicate a serious condition. You should isolate the guinea pig immediately. Do not to wait a day or so to see if things improve. Once the animal is isolated you can observe

Guinea pigs should always appear lively and alert. If you suspect your pet is ill, contact your veterinarian.

him more carefully. You can give him a thorough physical check and then place him in a warm environment. Telephone your vet and discuss the matter with him or her.

Injury

Injuries can range from a minor cut, to broken limbs, burns and any other wounds. Many diseases can be caused by secondary infection setting in to what might only be, initially, a minor lesion. Never leave skin abrasions untreated. They should be carefully washed, then treated with a suitable antiseptic powder, ointment or liquid. Exposed wounds are prime sites for bacterial colonization and infections. This will invariably result in a much more serious situation. The main causes of skin abrasions are scratches and minor cuts.

Incorrect Acclimation

When you acquire a guinea pig, bear in mind that when he changes

Causes of Stress

Stress is thought to be linked to the importance of elements in the guinea pig's environment that are needed for its general well being, but that are being denied to the animal. For example, any of the following may induce stress in your guinea pig: lack of space, incorrect diet, unclean housing, sudden and loud noises, excessive disturbance, lack of regular handling, changes in his environment, excessive heat or cold, bullying by other guinea pigs or pets, and lack of a retreat in the cage.

homes, it is probable that there will be some degree of change in the temperatures he is familiar with. If he came from a pet store or from a breeder whose housing was maintained at a higher temperature than the new accommodations, there would be every chance of him contracting a chill if you did not acclimatize him correctly. Any potential temperature differences should thus be considered and catered for. Acclimatization periods can range from a few days to a few weeks, depending on the type of accommodation and the time of the year.

Common Ailments

Now that you know what causes a guinea pig to become ill, let's take a brief look at some of the more common ailments.

Anal Fecal Impaction

When a guinea pig starts passing fewer or no droppings, this is a cause for concern. The muscles in the anus become weak, and the softer droppings build up in the skin fold until a painful lump forms. Bathroom habits of guinea pigs that have been impacted need to be monitored closely to make sure everything keeps working properly.

Bloody Urine

If your guinea pig is passing blood, he or she needs urgent veterinary attention. Bloody urine is never normal in guinea pigs, not even in sows, because they do not pass blood as part of their estrus cycle.

Diarrhea

Diarrhea results from an improper diet, sudden changes in the diet, illness, or infection. The vet should be contacted immediately. Never withhold water from the guinea pig, because dehydration will set in.

Eye Problems

Slight crustiness in the corner of the eye is common and can be gently cleaned away with a cotton swab dampened in water. Cloudy tears may sometimes appear in the corner of the eye when the guinea pig is cleaning his face or if a bit of dust has got into the eye. Excessive discharge, crustiness, cloudiness, weeping, or runny eyes

Guinea pigs can suffer from stress. Be sure to give your pet all the care and attention he deserves to keep him happy and healthy.

Guinea Pig Health Care

are cause for concern. This could indicate illness or injury, and medication may be needed.

Cataracts may occur in guinea pigs at any age, appearing as a cloudy film on the lens of the eyes. Sometimes only one eye is affected. If you think your guinea pig has a cataract, have him examined by a vet to make sure it is not some other eye illness or injury.

Foot and Leg Problems

If you see your guinea pig limping, pick him up and examine each of the legs for lumps, hot spots, and areas that cause the animal to wince when you touch them. Gently move the legs with your fingers. They should flex under your touch, not hang limply. If there does not appear to be anything wrong and the guinea pig is not in pain, then it is likely that a strain has occurred simply from the guinea pig twisting or moving his leg the wrong way. A guinea pig that "favors" a leg usually manages very well, and strains heal in a few days. However, consult your vet if the guinea pig is limping as the result of a trauma such as being dropped, or if he seems to be in pain.

Fungal Infections

Fungal infections such as ringworm can occur in guinea pigs and cause symptoms similar to parasitic infestations—the skin is dry, flaky, and irritated and there may be hair loss. Fungal infections are diagnosed by performing a fungal culture. Treatment varies from the use of topical ointments to oral medication. Care is needed when handling a guinea pig with a fungal infection until treatment is complete, because these infections can sometimes be passed on to humans.

Inner Ear Infection

A guinea pig suffering from an inner ear infection will exhibit extreme tilting of the head and have an overall miserable appearance. This painful condition requires immediate veterinary attention.

Abscesses

These occur periodically in guinea pigs, most commonly in the jaw area. Abscesses usually begin inside the mouth from a small cut or puncture caused by something the animal has eaten. The wound is seeded with bacteria and a hard lump filled with pus is formed. Abscesses may remain inside the mouth, but they usually work their way outward, creating a lump that is felt on the outside of the jaw, throat, or neck. An abscess must be lanced, drained, and flushed, and antibiotics are usually prescribed. Abscesses can also be found on other parts of a guinea pig as the result of bite wounds or scratches that have become infected. Guinea pigs with abscesses should be isolated from other animals until recovery is complete, because the bacteria are contagious.

Cysts

Sebaceous cysts, or pimples, can develop anywhere on a guinea pig's body. These must not be confused with abscesses—if in doubt, ask a professional. Sebaceous cysts are filled with white pus that does not smell bad. They squeeze out easily after the application of a compress made from a cloth dampened with warm water. Sebaceous cysts rarely become infected but should be watched closely until they are healed.

External Parasites

Guinea pigs can get fleas and lice, but only if they come in contact with another animal that already has these parasites. These pesky insects make their presence known by causing a guinea pig to scratch constantly. Small, white eggs may be found on the skin behind the ears, and adult lice can be seen attached to the skin or running about the scalp when the hair is parted. Bathing the guinea pig in an antiparasitic shampoo suitable for small animals treats lice and fleas. Some shampoos need to be left on for a few minutes in order to be effective. If this is the case, wrap the guinea pig in a towel to prevent him from licking at the shampoo and to keep him from becoming chilled. Do not use a flea powder, because it will cause eye and respiratory irritations.

Ear mites are only contracted through exposure to another pet that has them. If a guinea pig has ear mites, he will scratch, dig at his ears, and shake his head vigorously. There will be dirty-looking, crumbly earwax inside the ears. Prescription ear medication is required for treatment.

Skin mites burrow under the skin, causing redness, itchiness, swelling, and severe irritation. The skin appears dry and flaky, and the hair may come out in clumps. Skin mites are diagnosed by examining skin scrapings under a microscope and are treated with a series of injections of an antiparasitic agent.

Chances are that if one pet in your home has a parasite, the others will have it too. All your pets will need to be treated appropriately to prevent the spread and reoccurrence of parasites. Regular

Quick & Easy Guinea Pig Care

With the proper care, guinea pigs rarely become ill. However, you may wish to schedule a periodic veterinary checkup for your pet.

inspection of the skin should be done to check for parasites. All of these are easily eradicated with modern treatments.

Internal Parasites

Internal parasites, such as worms, can be identified via flotation methods and egg counts by your vet. Treatment is with vet-recommended drugs. General hygiene is the best preventive strategy in the control of parasites.

Ringworm is transmissible to humans and other animals. It is characterized by bald, reddened areas of skin that are flaky and encrusted. They may be on the face or body. Vet-recommended creams or other treatment should be effective, coupled with high standards of hygiene.

Superficial Wounds

Superficial wounds are caused by bites or accidental injuries and

Foot Problems

Pododermatitis, or "bumblefoot," is caused by bacteria that enter small lesions on the feet of guinea pigs that are housed on wire or other rough surfaces. The pads swell, blister, and become infected. This condition is managed by housing the animal on a clean, soft surface and by using an antibacterial ointment to soothe the skin. The actual swelling cannot be cured. Unsanitary conditions and allergies to bedding can also cause foot irritations. Foot problems are far more easily prevented than treated. Consult your veterinarian if you think your guinea pig has this condition.

should be treated with hydrogen peroxide or an antibacterial ointment to prevent infection. Wounds that are located on a spot that the guinea pig can reach to lick are best treated with peroxide rather than ointment because it dries quickly, leaving nothing to lick off.

Upper Respiratory Problems

Guinea pigs are highly susceptible to upper respiratory infections (URI), so they must be kept away from drafts, dampness, and fluctuating temperatures. This is also one of the major reasons for supplementing the diet with vitamin C. Symptoms include runny nose and eyes, shivering, coughing, sneezing, and labored breathing. If you think your guinea pig has a URI, keep him warm and seek veterinary attention. Guinea pigs do cough and sneeze occasionally, and there is no need to worry as long as these symptoms do not persist.

Dental Health

Guinea pig teeth are white in color, unlike those of other rodents, which are yellow. They have 20 teeth enclosed in their small jaws. There are four incisors in the front and inside the jaw, and on each side on both the top and bottom there are one premolar and three molars. Only the incisors are visible when you look at a guinea pig with his mouth slightly open. Overgrown teeth are a common problem in guinea pigs, and your veterinarian should perform oral examinations at least once a year. If any tooth faults are found, they can be corrected before the guinea pig has difficulty eating or damage to the jaw structure occurs. The molars are examined with an otoscope (the same instrument used by a vet to look inside the ears), which is inserted into the mouth.

Maintaining the Teeth

A guinea pig's teeth grow continuously, so your pet needs a constant supply of gnawing material in order to keep them pared down. Guinea pigs enjoy chewing on clean, dry twigs from trees (especially fruit trees), cardboard tubes from paper towel rolls, hay cubes, and food cubes. Guinea pigs should not be allowed to gnaw on soft plastic or vinyl items that are not digestible and could cause intestinal blockage.

Overgrown Incisors

In between regular vet exams, you should check your guinea pig's incisors. If the incisors become too long, your guinea pig will not be able to eat or use the water bottle properly. These teeth must be carefully trimmed back and the rough edges filed. Occasionally, a guinea pig will break one of his incisors, and although it will begin to regrow immediately, the rough edges should be filed and the matching tooth trimmed to the same length to make it easier for the animal to eat. Overgrown

Guinea pigs are loving, curious pets that are a delight to own. Provide your guinea pig with the necessary care and he will thank you for it for many years to come.

incisors are usually the result of a guinea pig not having enough hard things to gnaw on, but occasionally they can be indicative of a deeper problem within the molars and further investigation is warranted.

Malocclusion

Malocclusion is a devastating condition that occurs when the molars become overgrown. Normal top molars grow outward while the bottom molars grow inward, thus allowing them to meet and be worn down through the grinding of food. Malocclusion usually strikes the bottom molars, causing them to grow sideways and trap the tongue. Although heredity may predispose some guinea pigs to malocclusion, vitamin C deficiency is the more common cause. Symptoms include drooling, chewing difficulty, decreased food intake and output, or a complete inability to eat or drink. Veterinary attention is required at the first sign of this trouble. The molars have to be trimmed to allow the animal to return to his regular eating habits. Because the molars can always become overgrown again, any guinea pig that has had his teeth trimmed must have regular checkups.

Check Your Guinea Pig on a Regular Basis

In order to greatly reduce the incidence of disease or unhealthy conditions, it is worthwhile to take your guinea pig to the vet for periodic inspection. The vet may notice something you did not.

Diseases and other harmful conditions in guinea pigs can invariably be avoided by correct husbandry techniques. However, you can strengthen your general care regimen by regular physical examinations of your guinea pig. This should be done every time you handle him. By doing so, you will be able to spot problems before they get out of hand.